OCEANI
TRAVEL GUIDE
2024

Island Dreams: Your Comprehensive Oceania
Travel Handbook, Hidden Marvels Revealed,
Adventure, Exploration, Coastal, Pacific,
Culture, Cuisine, Landscapes, Local
Experience

Brandon Oliver

Brandon Oliver

TABLE OF CONTENTS

INTRODUCTION

Fellow travellers and adventure seekers! Buckle up for an exhilarating journey through the mesmerizing expanse of Oceania with our "Oceania Travel Guide 2024." This isn't just a book; it's your ticket to uncovering the heart and soul of the Pacific.

Picture this: turquoise waters lapping against pristine shores, ancient cultures telling tales as old as time, and landscapes that will leave you breathless. Our guide is here to be your trusty sidekick, guiding you through the myriad wonders of Oceania with insider tips and local insights.

Whether you're a backpacker with a knack for hidden gems or a luxury traveler seeking the perfect retreat, we've got you covered. Get into the vibrant cities, kick back on untouched beaches, and explore rainforests that seem straight out of a dream. Each chapter is crafted to let you tailor your adventure – after all, this journey is yours.

But it's not just about the touristy spots. We're all about those off-the-beaten-path discoveries. Meet the locals, savor the local flavors, and witness the magic of nature in places many might overlook.

Looking for practical advice? From cozy stays to culinary escapades and navigating local transport, our guide is loaded with tips to make your expedition seamless and unforgettable.

So, whether you're chasing thrills, soaking in culture, or just craving some R&R, Oceania is calling. Let the "Oceania Travel Guide 2024" be your compass, and let the Pacific weave its enchanting tale around you. Get ready for an odyssey that promises diversity, discovery, and memories that will last a lifetime!

CHAPTER 1

OVERVIEW OF OCEANIA

Oceania typically represent the vast expanse of the Pacific Ocean encompassing Australia, New Zealand, over a dozen Pacific Island Countries (PICs), and various dependencies, territories, and affiliated states, including Guam, American Samoa, Northern Marianas, and Midway. Encompassing nearly one-sixth of the Earth's surface, it serves as the strategic frontline between Asia and the Americas.

During the Cold War, spanning from 1945 to the early 1990s, Oceania was perceived as firmly aligned with the West, with significant American and British diplomatic and military involvement. However, after the Cold War, the region's strategic importance diminished in the eyes of the United States and the UK. Consequently, strategic oversight was largely delegated to the Five Eyes intelligence-sharing partners, Australia and New Zealand.

Recent years have witnessed a shift in interest, with Indonesia, Japan, India, and notably France intensifying their engagement with PICs. China, in particular, has become a disruptive force, leveraging soft loans, scholarships, immigration, commercial activities, military cooperation, and diplomacy to expand its influence in Oceania, even penetrating Australia and New Zealand's domestic affairs.

China's influence in Oceania carries global implications, contributing to tensions in the South and East China Seas. The PICs, forming the "third island chain," are crucial in China's ambition to limit U.S. influence, and discussions are underway with France to use French Polynesia as a strategic hub.

Besides geopolitical and geo-economics shifts, the region faces unprecedented geophysical changes, including severe weather events disrupting human security and economic activities. The convergence of these changes in the geopolitical, geo-economics, and geophysical spheres is complicating the strategic landscape in Oceania.

Australia and New Zealand are reassessing their roles in response to these transformations. New Zealand, for instance, has announced a Pacific reset to address strategic anxiety in Oceania and become a genuine partner for regional countries.

A crucial test case for this policy reset is the PACER Plus free trade agreement, hastily pushed through by Australia and New Zealand in 2017. However, its ratification remains pending, with PICs questioning its benefits and potential negative impacts on their economies. The outcome of the PACER Plus ratification process in 2018 will be indicative of whether Australia and New Zealand are truly committed to a policy reset or if they are prioritizing narrow domestic economic interests over regional growth and security, a model that has proven ineffective in the past.

Purpose of the travel guide

A Travel Guide, also known as a tour guide, tourist guide, or local guide, plays a crucial role in acquainting you with all the essential aspects to ensure a fulfilling experience at a destination. They excel at trip planning, creating a tailored experience by imparting insights and emphasizing the significance of the chosen destination. In today's fast-paced life, where many seek change and global exploration, some adopt a nomadic lifestyle. For others aiming to strike a balance, effective planning is essential for enjoyable and tranquil travels. A Tour Guide becomes indispensable in orchestrating, managing, and organizing the entire trip, allowing you to focus solely on relishing the destination while they handle all the logistics.

You are relieved of the burden of trip planning as Tour Guides manage all bookings and reservations, alleviating stress.

Their extensive network often translates to cost savings on hotels and tickets.

Tour Guides possess in-depth knowledge of the best attractions in each destination, ensuring you visit the most worthwhile places.

Exploring everything a location has to offer independently requires considerable time, effort, and courage. Tour Guides, familiar with the locale, prove invaluable in facilitating a wonderful and cost-effective trip.

They guarantee quality services and pay meticulous attention to ensuring your trip is satisfactory.

Contrary to a common misconception that hiring a tour guide may inflate your budget, the potential pitfalls of navigating a new place unassisted make their services a wise investment. Language barriers and unfamiliarity with local customs may leave you vulnerable to deception by locals. Tour Guides often speak multiple languages, such as English, German, French, Japanese, among others.

A Tour Guide assists with every aspect of your journey, from car rentals and hotel stays to exploring the surroundings, tailoring the experience to your preferences and providing accurate cost estimates.

CHAPTER 2

TRAVEL TIPS AND SAFETY INFORMATION

1. Prioritize Safety over Budget: Invest in your travel safety, especially when arriving late in a new country. Consider spending money on a taxi or staying in an airport hotel for added security.

Travel Safety Tip 1: Go for organized tour groups in potentially unsafe countries for a safer and well-planned experience.

2. Safeguard Your Money While Traveling: Wear a fanny pack or a money wallet to deter pickpockets. Carry your backpack on your chest in crowded places and be mindful of the amount of cash you have.

3. Dress Wisely for Travel Safety: Plan routes in advance, walk with confidence, and dress appropriately for cultural sensitivities. Avoid wearing expensive jewelry and inform your bank promptly if your phone or credit cards are lost or stolen.

Travel Safety Tip 2: Alert your bank or phone provider immediately to prevent unauthorized use.

4. Invest in Travel Insurance: Prioritize obtaining travel insurance to cover unforeseen expenses. Ensure coverage for medical emergencies, stolen belongings, or missed flights.

5. Exercise Caution in Choosing Dining Spots: Read restaurant reviews, choose popular establishments, and purify water using a water purifier. Be cautious with ice and salads, and consume peelable fruits to minimize the risk of bacterial contamination.

6. Research Local Scams for Enhanced Safety: Stay informed about potential scams in the area you're visiting. Seek tips from accommodation staff upon arrival.

Travel Safety Tip 3: Trust locals but exercise caution when dealing with strangers in unfamiliar places.

7. Familiarize Yourself with Safe Areas: Research government travel advice, including information on malaria, natural disasters, and safety recommendations for specific regions. Browse social media pages and traveler forums for insights and ask accommodation staff about neighborhoods to avoid.

8. Be Vigilant at ATMs: Exercise caution at ATMs, check for tampering, and ensure no one is watching you. Withdraw smaller amounts to minimize risks and use a travel cash card to avoid excessive fees.

Travel Safety Tip 4: Utilize a Wise Travel Money Card to bypass ATM fees and enhance financial security.

9. Never Leave Your Items Unattended:
Keep valuables close in the hold of planes, trains, or buses. Pack valuables in a small bag between your legs, doubling as a pillow during long trips. Padlock your bags with anti-theft material for added security.

10. Know Emergency Information: Write
down insurance details and local emergency numbers. Store information on your phone and on a paper in a protected cover. Keep copies and scans of important documents in case of theft.

11. Share Your Route with Your Family and Friends: Keep loved ones informed
about your travel route, especially in areas without wifi or phone signal. Consider using

the 'Find My Phone' feature for added security.

12. Don't just tell others where you're staying: Be cautious about sharing accommodation details until trust is established. Choose well-lit pickup locations for taxis to avoid potential scams. Use reputable taxi applications like Uber or Grab for trustworthy service.

13. Avoid Unnecessary Danger: Exercise caution and avoid unnecessary risks, such as straying from designated paths or engaging in unsafe activities. Prioritize safety, even when seeking adventurous experiences.

14. Being able to save yourself and others: Consider taking first-aid or language courses before traveling. For solo female travelers, a self-defense class can enhance personal safety.

15. Travel Safe in a Group: Enjoy the benefits of traveling in a group for added safety. Form connections in hostels or join organized tours to have extra eyes and ears for security.

16. Register with Your Embassy: Stay updated on warnings and advice by registering with your embassy. Facilitate quick assistance in emergencies, natural disasters, or passport-related issues.

17. Be Aware of Your Drink: Party responsibly, especially in unfamiliar places. Guard your drink, avoid leaving it unattended, and consider using a drink cover. Be mindful of alcohol strength variations in different countries and your personal tolerance, which may be affected by factors like altitude or heatstroke.

What's new in Oceania in 2024

1. Oceania Marina is set to undergo a significant refurbishment in May 2024. The refurbishment will introduce three new dining options: Aquamar Kitchen, a wellness-focused dining venue; an expanded poolside ice cream parlor offering inventive flavors from Humphry Slocombe; A recently opened relaxed outdoor trattoria offers delectable Italian cuisine, featuring freshly crafted pizzas. This refurbishment marks the completion of the fleet refurbishments for Oceania Cruises, resulting in a total of eight new or upgraded ships. The President of Oceania Cruises, Frank A. Del Rio, emphasized the ship's food-centric design, stating that Marina is designed and built for food enthusiasts. The ship's update includes three new dining venues, with a particular highlight on

expanding the popular Aquamar Kitchen concept.

Aquamar Kitchen, a signature restaurant, will feature wellness-inspired menus for breakfast and lunch, offering items such as smoothies, cold-pressed juices, avocado toast, salads, wraps, and heartier options. The restaurant's evening menu will include a transformation of Waves Grill into an al fresco trattoria, featuring freshly made pizzas, Italian specialties, and indulgent desserts.

In addition to the dining enhancements, Marina's private and public spaces will undergo refreshing updates to create a vibrant new ambiance. The upper suites, Polo Grill steakhouse, and Penthouse Suites will receive a revamped look, with redesigned features to enhance brightness and spaciousness. The refurbished ship is scheduled to debut on May 18, 2024, offering Mediterranean voyages exploring the region's history, cuisine, and traditions.

2. The Adventure Racing World Series in Oceania is expanding to include eight races presented by five experienced Race Directors, uniting Adventure Racing in Australia and New Zealand into a competitive race calendar. Teams participating in these races will be featured in the ARWS-Oceania rankings, with the X-Marathon 24-hour race at Lake Macquarie serving as the Oceania Championship, determining a team's qualification for the 2025 AR World Championship in Canada.

The series kicks off with Terra Nova, followed by Total Recon, Mountain Designs Geoquest, Hells Bells, X-Marathon as the Championship race, Wildside AR, Geoquest New Zealand, and concludes with the Top

Dog 24 race in the Australian Capital Territory.

Noteworthy additions to the series include the Total Recon race in South Australia and the return of adventure racing to the state after a long break. The X-Marathon, celebrating its 10th anniversary edition, serves as the 2024 ARWS Oceania Championship and offers the opportunity for the highest-ranked premier mixed team to qualify for the AR World Championship in Canada

The Wild side Adventure Race, celebrating its 10-year anniversary, returns to Forster, NSW, Australia, promising challenging treks, demanding mountain biking, and exciting paddling across three course options. The expansion of the Oceania Series is seen as a positive development by ARWS CEO Heidi Muller, anticipating an exciting year for adventure racing in the region with the passion and experience of the Race Directors ensuring an incredible racing experience in 2024.

CHAPTER 3

AUSTRALIA HIGHLIGHTS AND MUST-VISIT PLACES

Australia is a land of enchantment, as per Aboriginal mythology recounting the Dreamtime when celestial beings crafted its thriving coral reefs, lush rainforests, and red-earth deserts. Today, these vibrant ecosystems host some of the planet's most unique wildlife, drawing nature enthusiasts and adventurers worldwide.

Australia is also a realm of striking contradictions and breathtaking allure. Along the coastline, one can explore dynamic cities, expansive sand islands, and the awe-inspiring Great Barrier Reef—one of the world's natural wonders. In the Outback, rugged national parks and remote deserts beckon with rich Indigenous history.

Coupled with a laid-back atmosphere and amiable people, it's no wonder Australia consistently tops global bucket lists. Transform your travel dreams into reality by planning a visit to the country's top attractions.

Sydney Opera House, New South Wales: Mention Sydney, and the iconic Opera House comes to mind. Designed by Danish architect Jørn Utzon, this UNESCO World Heritage Site graces Sydney's Bennelong Point, surrounded by water on three sides and bordered by the Royal Botanic Gardens to the south. With its distinctive shell-like structure, the Opera House stands as a global architectural icon. While touring its interior is rewarding, the best views can be captured from Mrs Macquarie's Chair or a harbor cruise.

In 2023, the Sydney Opera House celebrates its 50th anniversary, featuring a calendar of special events and a newly renovated Concert Hall.

Great Barrier Reef Marine Park, Queensland: A must-see in Australia, the Great Barrier Reef is a UNESCO-listed marvel and one of the largest living structures globally, visible even from outer space. Established in 1975 to safeguard its fragile ecosystems, the marine park encompasses over 3,000 coral reefs, 600 continental islands, and inshore mangrove islands. Divers, snorkelers, and nature enthusiasts flock to witness it's astounding marine life, including diverse corals, tropical fish, sharks, dolphins, and turtles.

Various options exist for experiencing the Great Barrier Reef, from island cruises to snorkeling and diving tours departing from Cairns, Port Douglas, and Airlie Beach.

Uluru-Kata Tjuta National Park, Northern Territory: Deep in the Red Centre, Uluru stands as one of Australia's most photographed natural wonders. Rising 348 meters, it anchors Uluru-Kata Tjuta National Park, jointly managed by Parks Australia and the Anangu people. Kata Tjuta, striking red dome-shaped rocks, complements Uluru's beauty. Sunset offers prime viewing as the colors transform, and climbing Uluru was prohibited in 2019 out of respect for the traditional owners.

Sydney Harbour Bridge, New South Wales: Alongside the Opera House, the Sydney Harbour Bridge is an architectural marvel, known as "the Coathanger." Completed in 1932, it is the world's largest steel arch bridge, spanning 500 meters.

Visitors can embark on a guided ascent for panoramic views of the harbor and city, gaining a unique perspective of Sydney's layout.

Blue Mountains National Park, New South Wales: A UNESCO World Heritage Site, the Blue Mountains National Park, just 81 kilometers west of Sydney, offers a haven for hikers. Boasting dramatic gorges, waterfalls, and Aboriginal rock paintings, the park features iconic attractions like the Three Sisters rock formations. The Katoomba Scenic Railway, Skyway, Cableway, and Walkway provide elevated views, while various activities such as hiking, abseiling, and rock climbing cater to adventure seekers.

Melbourne's Culture, Victoria: Melbourne, Australia's second-largest city, charms culture enthusiasts with its galleries, theaters, and European ambiance. The National Gallery of

Victoria, Arts Centre Melbourne, and Federation Square showcase artistic endeavors. Nature lovers can follow the Aboriginal Heritage Walk at the Royal Botanic Gardens, and sports enthusiasts can catch a game at the Melbourne Cricket Ground. Rich in history, Melbourne also boasts grand Victorian buildings and elegant arcades, reflecting its Gold Rush past.

Bondi Beach, New South Wales: Known for its bronzed bodies and iconic surf culture, Bondi Beach, a short drive from Sydney, is a world-renowned destination. Beyond its golden sands, visitors can explore the Bondi to Bronte coastal walk, attend Sunday markets, or dine with a view at the famous Icebergs dining room. Bondi hosts one of the oldest Surf Life Saving Clubs, and caution is advised due to strong rip tides.

Daintree National Park, Queensland:

Daintree National Park, a Wet Tropics World Heritage Area in Far North Queensland, reveals one of the Earth's most ancient ecosystems. Encompassing Mossman Gorge and Cape Tribulation, where rainforest meets reef, the park showcases remarkable biodiversity. Guided safaris from the resort town of Port Douglas offer immersive experiences, allowing visitors to encounter unique species like the cassowary, crocodile, Ulysses butterfly, and Bennett's tree kangaroo.

K'Gari (Fraser Island), Queensland:

K'Gari, or Fraser Island, holds a distinguished place among Australia's unique destinations. Situated off the east coast between Bundaberg and Brisbane, it claims the title of the world's largest sand island. Endless sandy stretches, turquoise lakes, emerald rainforests, and diverse wildlife characterize this remarkable location.

For thrill-seekers, a 4WD journey along its surf-battered shores is a premier outdoor adventure. Seventy Five Mile Beach offers views of shipwrecks, the colored cliffs of The Cathedrals, and Champagne Pools, natural rock pools filled with bubbling fish.

Inland exploration unveils crystal-clear freshwater creeks, lakes surrounded by towering sand dunes, and ancient rainforests boasting diverse flora and fauna. Sharks, dolphins, and whales inhabit the surrounding waters, while dingoes, bats, sugar gliders, and over 300 bird species thrive on land.

Nature enthusiasts can partake in whale watching, sunset cruises, rainforest hikes at Central Station, floating down Eli Creek, or scenic flights over the stunning landscapes. Accessible by ferry from Rainbow Beach and

Hervey Bay, Fraser Island demands 4WD vehicles due to its lack of sealed roads.

Kakadu National Park, Northern Territory: Kakadu National Park stands as an exemplar of Australia's wilderness, spanning over 19,840 square kilometers in the Northern Territory—ranking as the world's second-largest national park. This diverse landscape encompasses monsoon rainforests, mangrove swamps, rivers, gorges, ancient rock paintings, wetlands, and waterfalls.

The park's biodiversity is showcased through over 300 bird species, various mammals, reptiles, and both freshwater and saltwater crocodiles. Cruises along waterways, hiking trails, and scenic flights offer immersive experiences in exploring Kakadu's ecosystems.

Accessible from Darwin during the dry season, which runs approximately three hours by car, some areas may close during the wet season (Nov-April) due to heavy flooding. Nonetheless, the wet season brings out the best in waterfalls and wetlands.

Great Ocean Road, Victoria: Renowned as one of the world's premier scenic drives, the Great Ocean Road stretches 300 kilometers along Australia's rugged southeast coast. Originating as a Depression-era project, it winds along plunging sea cliffs from Torquay to Allansford near Warrnambool.

Port Campbell National Park, a highlight along the route, features natural wonders like the Twelve Apostles, London Bridge, the Arch, and Loch Ard Gorge. These wind- and wave-sculpted rock formations create a mesmerizing puzzle adrift along the coast.

Beyond the geological marvels, activities along the Great Ocean Road include visiting the Australian National Surfing Museum, surfing at Bells Beach, exploring seaside resorts like Lorne, and whale watching in Warrnambool. Nature enthusiasts can delve into eucalyptus forests, fern-filled rainforests, and hiking trails in Otway National Park.

Broome, Western Australia: Once the pearl capital, Broome in Western Australia has transformed into a thriving tourist town and a gateway to the spectacular Kimberley region. Cable Beach, with its endless white sands and turquoise waters, stands as a star attraction, offering camel rides at sunset.

Town Beach hosts the Staircase to the Moon phenomenon between March and October, creating an illusion of steps leading to the moon. Other highlights include the red cliffs of Gantheaume Point and the Malcolm Douglas Crocodile Park.

Historical and cultural attractions abound, from the Broome Historical Museum to watching movies under star-studded skies at Sun Pictures. Pearl farm tours, whale watching, and Kimberley adventures further enrich the Broome experience.

Kangaroo Island, South Australia: Nature takes center stage on Kangaroo Island, off South Australia's Fleurieu Peninsula. Kangaroos hop along powdery shores, sea lions and penguins frolic in crystal-clear waters, and koalas cling to fragrant eucalyptus trees. Diving enthusiasts can explore temperate waters with sea dragons and shipwrecks. Natural wonders like the Remarkable Rocks and Admirals Arch in Flinders Chase National Park showcase wind-sculpted rock formations. Hiking trails along sea cliffs, through forests, and exploring cave systems provide opportunities to encounter unique wildlife.

To access Kangaroo Island, travelers can fly directly from Adelaide or take a ferry from Cape Jervis on the Fleurieu Peninsula.

Cradle Mountain-Lake St. Clair National Park, Tasmania: Cradle Mountain-Lake St. Clair National Park in Tasmania captivates nature lovers with its sparkling lakes, serrated peaks, alpine heathland, and dense forests. Home to Mount Ossa, Tasmania's highest point, the park offers fantastic hiking trails, including the Weindorfer Walk and Lake Dove Walk, with breathtaking vistas of Cradle Mountain.

Wildlife enthusiasts can spot Tasmanian devils, wombats, wallabies, pademelons, and platypus in this glacier-carved wilderness. Experienced hikers may undertake the famous

80-kilometer Overland Track, and the park provides an immersive experience into Tasmania's diverse flora and fauna.

Horizontal Falls & the Kimberley Region: The Kimberley region in Australia's northwest unfolds as a remote and rugged expanse of red rocks, gorges, deserts, and cliff-fringed coasts. Among its highlights is the breathtaking Horizontal Falls, where powerful tides rush through narrow gorges. Travelers can board jet boats for an exhilarating ride through this natural wonder.

Broome serves as the gateway to the Kimberley, offering opportunities to explore scarlet sea cliffs, visit pearl farms, and embark on 4WD safaris along the Gibb River Road. Mitchell Falls, Purnululu National Park (Bungle Bungle), and the Argyle Diamond mine add to the region's spectacular allure.

Train Trips across the Outback: Traversing the Outback becomes a seamless adventure through luxurious train journeys. The Indian Pacific, Australia's longest train trip, spans Perth, Adelaide, and Sydney over four days, highlighting Blue Mountains, Pink Lakes of South Australia, Nullabor Plain, and culinary experiences.

The Ghan offers iconic train trips with routes including Adelaide to Darwin, Adelaide to Alice Springs, and Darwin to Alice Springs, traversing remote areas like Coober Pedy and the Flinders Ranges. For a shorter journey, the Spirit of the Outback covers Brisbane to Longreach in 26 hours, passing through heritage mining towns and the Stockmen's Hall of Fame.

These train trips provide a unique perspective on Australia's vast and diverse landscapes, making it an ideal way to explore multiple attractions in one memorable journey.

Australia cities and regions

Australia, the world's largest island and smallest continent, is a diverse country divided into six states and two territories. Each region has its own charm, offering a unique blend of landscapes, cultures, and lifestyles. Whether you're into thrilling adventures, relaxing beach vibes, exquisite wine, or family-friendly activities, there's something for everyone across the country.

Let's examine each state more closely:

New South Wales (NSW): From indulgent wine regions to pristine seaside villages and mountain wilderness, NSW is a versatile destination. Sydney, the bustling capital, stands on the shores of Port Jackson, offering a dynamic urban experience. With the Sapphire Coast, Central Coast, and Blue

Mountains, NSW caters to thrill-seekers, beach lovers, wine connoisseurs, and families alike.

Northern Territory (NT): Home to Darwin, the capital city, NT takes the outback experience to new heights. Premier national parks like Kakadu, King's Canyon, and Litchfield, along with the iconic Uluru, showcase quintessential Australia stunning landscapes, iconic wildlife, and authentic Aboriginal culture.

Queensland (QLD): Known as the Sunshine State, QLD on the northeast is a paradise for sun-loving, beach-goers. The Great Barrier Reef, Daintree Rainforest, and Whitsunday Islands are treasures. Brisbane, the state's capital, enjoys abundant sunshine, making it perfect for outdoor activities and water sports.

South Australia (SA): Nestled in the central part, SA is a laid-back destination, ideal for a relaxing getaway. Adelaide, the capital, serves as a great base for exploring wineries in the Barossa Valley, Flinders Ranges, and Kangaroo Island. SA, the 'Festival State,' hosts over 500 events and festivals annually.

Tasmania (TAS): Separated by the Bass Strait, TAS is a microcosm of Australia, offering dazzling beaches, rugged mountains, and picturesque landscapes. Hobart, the capital, is a cosmopolitan city near regional towns, known for food and wine trails, family activities, and breathtaking walks.

Victoria (VIC): Melbourne, the cultural heart of Australia, is in VIC. The state boasts incredible museums, galleries, the Grampians National Park, and the Great Ocean Road. Its cultural diversity, modern cityscape, and friendly atmosphere make it a vibrant destination.

Western Australia (WA): The largest state on the west coast offers diverse attractions, from the dramatic Kimberley Region to the idyllic Rottnest Island. Perth, the capital, is famous for serene beaches, parklands, and fresh seafood, making it an appealing destination for relaxation.

Australian Capital Territory (ACT): Canberra, the nation's capital, blends nature and culture seamlessly. With monuments, museums, glistening lakes, and wild wetlands, ACT has a cosmopolitan atmosphere and modern appeal. It houses significant national institutions, a flourishing restaurant scene, and beautiful parks and gardens.

External Territories: Australia administers various external territories, including Ashmore and Cartier Islands, Christmas Island, Cocos Islands, Jervis Bay Territory, Coral Sea Islands, Heard and McDonald Islands, Norfolk Island, and the Australian Antarctic Territory, covering 42% of the Antarctic continent. Each of these territories adds to the richness and diversity of Australia's overall landscape.

Australia outdoor adventures

Australia, a vast and enticing landmass at the bottom of the globe, conjures up images of raw, sunburnt earth and pristine sands, inviting adventure seekers to explore its wonders. Whether it's the magical allure of wilderness, the carefree moments on bronzed beaches, or the camaraderie of late-night kebabs, the call of adventure in Australia is impossible to resist.

Australia's best experiences go beyond its natural beauty, offering a unique blend of weird, wonderful, and wild adventures. Backpacking through the country is a journey filled with experiences that are distinctly 'down-under.' From trying Vegemite for the first time to encountering the scaly local inhabitants, every moment is a chance to embrace the extraordinary.

As you embark on this wild ride, be prepared for a uniquely Australian vocabulary. By the end of your journey, you'll be fluent in the language of the down under, both figuratively and literally if your dictionary happens to be a local.

Van life and the Great Australian Dream: Before solar panels and trendy van conversions, there existed a simple breed of Australians roaming the coastlines in beat-up Kombi vans. The tradition of van life has evolved into a shared dream for many, from adventurous backpackers to seasoned nomads. Exploring the best of Australia often involves chasing sunsets on the West Coast, catching sunrises on the East Coast, and, of course, enjoying the freedom of the open road.

For those seeking a hassle-free road trip, van rentals equipped for outback adventures are the ways to go. Buckle up, and you're ready for the ultimate Australian journey.

Traversing the Continent an Initiation Journey: Driving across the vast expanse of Australia is a classic adventure, a rite of passage for those seeking the extraordinary. With spectacular drives linking the coasts, the journey from one side to the other becomes an adventure in itself. Whether following the Great Ocean Road or venturing through the Nullarbor Plain, the experience is nothing short of epic. Driving six days straight through the Outback with only roadkill for company is an essential Australian travel tale.

Gone Walkabout – Best Adventures in Australia's Hiking Trails: For the truly adventurous, ditching the car and embracing hiking trails is the way to lose yourself in the Australian wilderness. From the first men to the modern swagmen, bushwalking is a time-honored Aussie adventure. With the right backpacking gear, the opportunities for bushwalking are limitless. Australia's national parks, encompassing diverse landscapes, offer hiking trails that cater to all levels of adventurers.

Noteworthy trails include the Blue Mountains National Park in New South Wales, the Daintree Rainforest in Queensland, the Grampians (or 'Gramps') in Victoria, the Simpson Desert in South Australia, Kakadu National Park in the Northern Territory,

Nambung National Park in Western Australia, and Cradle Mountain-Lake St Clair National Park in Tasmania. Each state presents a unique outdoor playground waiting to be explored.

Get Outdoors – Exploring Australia's National Parks: Fresh from compiling the ultimate list of Australia's finest national parks, I'm now armed with a treasure trove of nature-related tidbits about Oz! For instance, did you know that the Greater Blue Mountains Area, spanning seven national parks and one conservation area, is approximately one-third the size of Belgium? Or that Fraser Island holds the title of the world's largest sand island? And let's not forget the discovery of one of the oldest ritual burials on the desolate shores of New South Wales's Lake Mungo.

Enough of these intriguing, nerdy facts —
they're sure to impress both spunky sheilas
and cuddly blokes at the local pub! One
captivating image is all it takes to make you a
believer in the irreverent magnificence of
Australia's outdoor havens. Whether you
fancy hiking, mountain biking, rock climbing,
or simply driving to the best viewpoints,
Australia's national parks offer an
unforgettable experience.

Here are my top picks by state:

**New South Wales – Blue Mountains
National Park**: A natural wonder, the Blue
Mountains National Park in New South Wales
boasts rugged cliffs, deep valleys, and the
iconic Three Sisters rock formation. It's a
haven for hikers and nature enthusiasts
seeking breathtaking vistas.

Queensland – Daintree Rainforest:
Queensland's Daintree Rainforest is a UNESCO World Heritage site, home to a diverse range of flora and fauna. With lush greenery, crystal-clear streams, and unique wildlife, it's a paradise for those seeking an immersive rainforest experience.

Victoria – The Grampians (bonus points for calling them 'Gramps'):

The Grampians, affectionately known as 'Gramps,' offers stunning sandstone mountains, vibrant wildflowers, and ancient Aboriginal rock art. It's a haven for outdoor activities, including hiking, rock climbing, and wildlife spotting.

South Australia – Simpson Desert: For an outback adventure, the Simpson Desert in South Australia beckons with its mesmerizing red dunes and vast landscapes. It's a remote and challenging destination, perfect for those seeking a true desert experience.

Northern Territory – Kakadu National Park: Kakadu National Park is a treasure trove of natural and cultural wonders. From wetlands teeming with wildlife to ancient Aboriginal rock art, it offers a diverse and rich experience for nature lovers and history enthusiasts alike.

Western Australia – Nambung National Park: Nambung National Park is famous for the otherworldly Pinnacles Desert, where eerie limestone formations rise from the golden sands. It's a surreal landscape, perfect for exploration and photography.

Tasmania – Cradle Mountain-Lake St Clair National Park: Tasmania's Cradle Mountain-Lake St Clair National Park is a pristine wilderness with alpine landscapes, ancient rainforests, and the iconic Cradle Mountain. It's a hiker's paradise, offering various trails for all skill levels.

Mad Max, Eat Your Heart Out – The Best Australian 4×4 Trips: Venturing into some of Australia's most stunning locations often requires more than just your standard vehicle. There are hidden gems inaccessible without a robust 4WD and countless unsealed roads in the outback that demand off-road capabilities. While Australians traditionally engage in 4WD adventures with a touch of high spirits or spirits themselves, embarking on this journey requires a sober approach with ample water, preparation, and, of course, sexy backpacker insurance.

Once you're out there, it's like stepping into a theme park – from deep-cut cavernous gorges to rolling red dunes in the desert expanses. Whether exploring national parks, the spaces in between, or the vastness of Western Australia, welcome to the Thunder dome.

While the popular Gibb River Road in the unreal Kimberly Region offers a quintessential 4×4 adventure, the Canning Stock Route provides a meaty challenge for those seeking remote experiences. The Victorian High Country, a significantly shorter drive, offers a different perspective on the Outback's sights.

Really Going Down Under – Scuba Diving in Australia's Waters: Six entries in, and we're finally diving into the beaches, the heart of any island paradise. Forget Bondi Beach; the real adventure lies beneath the waves. Enter the Great Barrier Reef, the world's longest coral reef and a UNESCO World Heritage site, stretching nearly the entire length of Queensland's eastern coast. Dive into a world of vibrant marine life, tropical fish, and serene oceanic landscapes.

Scuba diving territories along the Queensland coastline, especially around Cairns, Townsville, and Port Douglas, offer spectacular underwater experiences. Beyond Queensland, Ningaloo Reef in Western Australia provides a golden opportunity to dive with diverse marine life, including majestic whale sharks. For a truly untouched experience, head to Christmas Island or Lord Howe Island.

Australia isn't just a magnificent diving destination; it's also one of the best places for a liveaboard trip globally. With expansive dive territories and endless coastlines, living on-site at the dive site becomes the ultimate adventure vacation in Australia. Eat, sleep, dive, repeat – that's the name of the game. Don't miss out on booking a live aboard trip to witness the unfathomable beauty of the Great Barrier Reef.

Grommet to Grouse – Livin' the Surfie Life: Amidst the heavenly strips of sand, surfing takes center stage as one of the top things to do in Australia. From the hedonistic east coast experience in Cairns, the Gold Coast, Surfers Paradise, to the classic backpacker haven Byron Bay – surfing towns are epic destinations. However, for the true surf enthusiasts seeking bigger waves and wilder tides, the Margaret River area on the west coast is the place to be. Keen surfers should also check out Bell's Beach in Victoria, the location of the annual Rip Curl Pro event.

Surfers live the dream, waking up (probably in a van), surfing, and indulging in a big breakfast, snoozing, surfing again, maybe a joint, another snooze, and afternoon surf. The surf culture is not just a lifestyle; it's an adventure, and surfeits get a fair share of excitement, not to mention more frequent social interactions than their bushwalking counterparts.

Party like a Feral: While many Australian adventures happen under the sun, not all of them require the sweltering heat. Australians are renowned for their adventurous palate, sticking just about anything in their mouths. The real parties, however, unfold outside – in the Australian outdoors.

Enter 'doofs,' the bass-induced hippy festivals of psy, dub, glitch, and bud. Rainbow Serpent may be the biggest in this style, but for a truly stellar experience, head to Queensland. From multi-stage madness to one-stage fun and regional burns, things are bound to get weird. The ferals know how to get loose, and Aussies, among them, are some of the loosest cannons, with booze flowing and bud blazing.

While traditional music festivals like the Byron Bay Blues fest are noteworthy, the true Australian party experience involves 'doofing.'

Shouting out the Best Adventures in Australia for the Indoors Lovers: Who needs fresh air when you can have air-con? For those who prefer the concrete jungle over outdoor escapades, Australia still offers cool places to explore. While not heart-pounding or jaw-dropping, these snippets of Aussie culture provide adventures in their own right:

• **Melbourne's Laneways:** Winding alleyways of street art, velvety jazz lounges, and chic hole-in-the-walls define Melbourne's cool factor.

• **Museum of Old and New Art (MONA):** Located in Hobart, MONA amplifies low-key cultural goodness through insane exhibitions, earning it the title of a "subversive adult Disneyland.

• **Breweries, Wineries, and Booze:** Australians drink a lot, and the country is home to fantastic breweries, craft, and big-time, as well as renowned wine regions.

• **Aboriginal Ceremonies:** Seek out performances of traditional Aboriginal ceremonies for insight into the first Australians' culture.

Shouting out the Best Outdoor Adventures in Australia: Now, let's head in the opposite direction – away from the stuffy air-coned galleries and into the realm of action:

• **Skydiving:** With numerous locations, including over Uluru, skydiving in Australia offers breathtaking views above the scarlet sands of Central Australia.

• **Bungee Jumping:** Stay in Cairns for this Queenstown-esque adventure hub with a variety of thrilling offerings.

• **Abseiling:** Explore steep cliffs in places like the Blue Mountains National Park, combining abseiling with cannoning and rock climbing for a memorable adventure.

• **White Water Rafting:** Choose between the Tully River and the Barron River, both near Cairns, for year-round rafting hotspots with various rapids.

Australia is undoubtedly one of the best places for adventure travel, offering a plethora of outdoor activities for thrill-seekers and nature enthusiasts alike.

CHAPTER 4

DISCOVER THE ENCHANTING REALM OF THE LONG WHITE CLOUD IN NEW ZEALAND

Māori Cultural Experiences in New Zealand

1. Meet the Descendants of Kupe, Northland: In the vibrant community of Kupe, Northland, visitors can immerse themselves in the living Maori culture. Manea Footprints of Kupe, situated on the shores of Hokianga Harbour, narrates the first chapter of New Zealand's human history. This cultural encounter explores prehistoric tribal narratives, Māori spiritual beliefs, and the impact of Pākehā (Europeans). The community takes great pride in celebrating its history and traditions daily, making it easy for visitors to feel at home.

2. Stand In The Shade Of An Ancient Forest Giant, Northland: The ancient forests of Northland, with their towering kauri trees, offer a unique and biodiverse experience. Waipoua Forest, home to the famous Tane Mahuta, provides an awe-inspiring encounter with these ancient giants. Standing in the shade of these trees offers a glimpse into the beauty and diversity of New Zealand's natural landscapes.

3. Visit the Birthplace of Today's New Zealand, Northland: The Waitangi Treaty Grounds in Northland provide a cultural and historical experience centered on the Treaty of Waitangi. Visitors can engage in traditional Maori activities, witness cultural performances, and learn about the history and significance of this treaty, offering a unique and enriching experience for all.

4. Rotorua's Geothermal Wonder and Māori Art in Action: Only in New Zealand: Te Puia and the Whakarewarewa Geothermal Valley in Rotorua showcase Maori culture, history, and geothermal wonders. The Whakarewarewa geothermal area features bubbling mud pools, geysers, and steam vents, providing a natural spectacle. Te Puia also houses the New Zealand Māori Arts and Crafts Institute, preserving and promoting traditional Maori arts and crafts through live demonstrations and workshops.

Experience the Home of Middle-earth: New Zealand, known as the home of Middle-earth, offers visitors the opportunity to explore the stunning landscapes featured in J.R.R. Tolkien's "The Lord of the Rings" trilogy. Popular film locations include:

Hobbit on Movie Set: permanent movie set in Matamata, where visitors can tour hobbit holes, Bag End, and the Green Dragon Inn.

Mount Ngauruhoe: An active volcano in Tongariro National Park, serving as Mount Doom in the films. Explorers have the opportunity to trek the Tongariro Alpine Crossing.

Kaitoke Regional Park: The location for Rivendell, the elven sanctuary in the films, near Upper Hutt.

Queenstown: Used in several films, including Isengard and the Ford of Bruinen.

This journey allows visitors to experience the enchanting world of Middle-earth and relive the magic of the films.

New Zealand's Distinctive and Unique Luxury Lodges:

New Zealand boasts several luxury lodges offering a five-star experience in remote and beautiful locations:

The Lodge at Kauri Cliffs near Matauri Bay:

Set near Matauri Bay, this lodge is perfect for active travelers who appreciate luxury. The David Harman-designed golf course provides stunning views of the Pacific.

Huka Lodge near Lake Taupō: As one of the world's most revered luxury accommodations, Huka Lodge has an impressive heritage and has hosted influential guests, including the Queen, Mick Jagger, Bill Gates, and Barbra Streisand. Situated near Lake Taupō, it offers a luxurious and inspirational retreat.

These lodges offer top-notch amenities and services, ensuring an unforgettable stay in New Zealand's most beautiful and remote areas.

Attractions of north and south islands in New Zealand

Must-See Destinations on New Zealand's South Island:

Queenstown

Located on the shores of Lake Wakatipu, surrounded by stunning mountain peaks, including The Remarkables Mountain Range. Offers a variety of attractions, including hiking trails, adventure activities, hot pools, wineries, and bike trails. Ideal for family-friendly activities like Lake Wakatipu scenic cruises or evening dinner and cruise experiences. Perfect launchpad to explore other South Island destinations.

Milford Sound

Famous fiord carved by glaciers, featuring steep cliffs and unique marine life. A must-visit destination with options for sightseeing cruises, kayaking, hiking, and scenic flights. Consider a full-day tour from Queenstown, offering a guided journey with stops at Mirror Lakes, Lake Marian, Pop's View Lookout, and The Chasm. Overnight cruise experiences available for a more immersive and unforgettable visit.

Te Anau

Situated on the shores of Lake Te Anau, offering attractions like glow-worm caves, Doubtful Sound, and the Kepler Track. Te Anau glow-worm cave tour provides a magical underground experience with a cruise across Lake Te Anau. Hike the Kepler Track, one of New Zealand's Great Walks, offering a 60-kilometer loop track or a day hike to Luxmore Hut. Explore Milford Sound from Te Anau with guided tours and scenic cruises.

Mount Cook National Park

Home to Aoraki/Mount Cook, New Zealand's tallest mountain, surrounded by alpine lakes, glaciers, and hiking trails. Mueller Hut hike offers breathtaking views of Mount Cook, Hooker Lake, Mueller Lake, and Mueller Glacier. Scenic helicopter tours provide an aerial perspective of the stunning landscapes. Ideal for outdoor enthusiasts seeking a paradise on earth.

Glenorchy

A scenic 45-minute drive from Queenstown to a small town surrounded by pristine landscapes and wilderness. Outdoor adventures include the Glenorchy Walkway, Routeburn track hiking, and jet boating tours.

Scenic drive along Lake Wakatipu with stops at Moke Lake, Bob's Cove Track, and Bennetts Bluff Lookout. Half-day tours from Queenstown to Glenorchy offer viewpoints, Lord of the Rings filming locations, and lakeside picnics.

These destinations showcase the diverse and breathtaking landscapes of the South Island, providing a range of outdoor activities and memorable experiences for visitors.

Arrow town

Arrow town, a former gold mining village, still gleams with its historical charm despite the end of mining activities. Unlike many other New Zealand towns, Arrow town has preserved much of its old architecture, offering not just visual appeal but also numerous opportunities for captivating photos.

Located just a short 15-minute drive northeast of Queenstown, you can reach Arrow town by public bus, bike trail, or guided tour. Opting for a guided tour ensures a seamless experience with various enjoyable activities. With transportation included and a maximum of 11 people per tour, it feels personalized, allowing you to ask questions and connect with fellow participants. Tickets start at $209 NZD per person, so make sure to check availability and book in advance, as this tour is quite popular.

For wine enthusiasts, there's a hop-on hop-off wine tour bus from Queenstown to explore Arrow town and the top wineries in the region. Choose between a half-day or full-day tour, with tickets priced at $65.50 NZD and $89.50 NZD, respectively. With transportation covered, it's a fantastic opportunity to savor some exceptional wines.

Once in Arrow town, take a leisurely stroll along the main street for shopping and consider dining at the well-known Slow Cuts restaurant for a delicious meal and craft beer. If time permits, a walk along the Arrow River, a visit to the Old Chinese Settlement or a short hike on trails like Big Hill, Sawpit Gully Track, and Tobins Track are all delightful options. Arrow town offers a range of activities, making it a tempting choice for an overnight stay!

Wanaka

When contemplating a permanent move to New Zealand, I faced the tough decision between Wanaka and Queenstown. Both hold a special place in my heart, but ultimately, Queenstown won. Nevertheless, Wanaka remains one of my favorite South Island towns.

Nestled on the shores of Lake Wanaka, often regarded as New Zealand's most beautiful lake, Wanaka offers breathtaking views with fewer crowds compared to Queenstown. A simple joy for me is grabbing a coffee and taking a leisurely stroll along the lake, reveling in its beauty.

For those seeking free activities, hiking Roy's Peak is a must, providing stunning views from the famous viewpoint. Alternatively, a drive to Mt Aspiring National Park to visit Diamond Lake offers a shorter hike. Paid activities include a thrilling jet boat ride on the Clutha River for adrenaline enthusiasts or a more relaxed wine and cheese cruise on Lake Wanaka, starting right in town.

Wanaka is also proud to claim the title of the craft beer capital of New Zealand, boasting more breweries per capita than anywhere else in the country. Rhyme and Reason Brewery, with its fantastic IPAs and pale ales, is a personal favorite. If you enjoy drinks, consider spending at least one night in Wanaka to fully appreciate its offerings.

Doubtful Sound

For those craving off-the-beaten-path adventures, Doubtful Sound serves as the perfect alternative to Milford Sound. As the largest fiord in Fordland National Park, Doubtful Sound competes fiercely with Milford Sound in terms of awe-inspiring scenery.

While not far from Te Anau, reaching Doubtful Sound involves an adventure, accessible only through organized tours from Queenstown or Manapouri. The journey includes a bus to Te Anau, a ferry across Lake Manapouri, and another bus into Doubtful Sound, followed by a scenic boat trip. The tour duration is around 7 hours from Manapouri and approximately 12 hours from Queenstown.

Consider an overnight cruise in Doubtful Sound for a unique experience, waking up to stunning views with fewer crowds. A 3-day tour includes an overnight cruise, a visit to the Te Anau Glow Worm Caves, and a second night in a nearby hotel. Alternatively, a one-night overnight tour offers spectacular sunrise views at a slightly lower cost.

Deciding between Milford Sound and Doubtful Sound depends on your preferences. If you enjoy a busier atmosphere, Milford Sound is ideal, while those seeking rugged adventures may favor Doubtful Sound. Why not experience both if time allows?

Gibbston Valley

My preferred wine region in New Zealand is Gibbston Valley, conveniently located just 25 minutes from Queenstown. Renowned for its Pinot Noir, Pinot Gris, Rose, Riesling, Sauvignon Blanc, and Chardonnay, the valley offers a rich array of delightful wines.

All the wineries in Gibbston Valley are boutique, making their wines exclusive. Taking home a bottle or three becomes the perfect souvenir. Explore the valley on a wine tour from Queenstown, with options for full or half-day tours, including a visit to various wineries and a pleasant lunch.

The tour, priced at $289 NZD per person, provides an exceptional foodie experience, pairing multiple wines with dishes. While most tours cost around $200+ NZD, budget-friendly options like the hop-on-hop-off wine tour, priced at $65.50 NZD per person, are available. Keep in mind that tasting fees are usually waived when purchasing a bottle from the wineries.

For an extended experience, consider spending the night in Gibbston Valley, with Kinross Cottages being a popular choice. Positioned right by the cellar door of five boutique wineries, it offers a perfect location. Enjoy as much wine as you like before retreating to your luxurious cottage for a romantic getaway in New Zealand!

The Blue Pools

Traveling down the wild adventure of the South Island's West Coast leads to incredible stops, with one of the highlights being the Blue Pools, just north of Wanaka.

Embark on a short walk across two suspension bridges to witness the mesmerizing blue hues of New Zealand's possibly bluest river. In summer, the calm pool transforms into a popular swimming spot, offering breathtaking views from both above and the beach below.

The nearest town, Makarora, is a convenient 6-minute drive from the Blue Pools parking lot. It's the ideal base to avoid crowds when visiting this exceptional attraction. Accommodation options are limited in Makarora, with the Makarora Mountain View and Wonderland Makarora Lodge being the two choices. Both offer cabins and chalets, with Makarora Mountain View providing a more luxurious option.

A visit to the Blue Pools ranks among the best experiences on the South Island, and staying in Makarora allows you to enjoy this gem without the hustle and bustle. Just remember to pack plenty of bug spray to ward off the persistent black flies!

New Zealand north island attractions

So, you're embarking on a journey through the North Island of New Zealand, also known as Te Ika-a-Māui. Wondering about the absolute must-dos? Well, here's a handy compilation to make planning your trip a breeze. From captivating geothermal wonders and immersive Maori culture to the delightful world of aromatic wines, the North Island has a plethora of experiences waiting for you.

1. Get up close with New Zealand's emblematic Kiwi Bird

Witness the flightless wonder, the kiwi, at one of the various conservation centers on the North Island, such as the National Kiwi Hatchery in Rotorua or the Otorohanga Kiwi House.

2. Head as far north as you can go in New Zealand to Cape Reinga

Make a pit stop at the iconic lighthouse marking the (almost) northern tip of the North Island. Whether you drive there independently or join a tour for some sandboarding on Ninety Mile Beach, it's a photo-worthy adventure.

3. Immerse yourself in Maori culture with a Hangi Dinner

Get into New Zealand's rich Maori heritage with an evening village tour in Rotorua. Both Mitai Maori Village and Te Pa Tu (formerly Tamaki Maori Village) offer engaging experiences with performances, mini-workshops, and a traditional hangi meal.

4. Trek to the Pouakai Mirror Lakes

Explore the breathtaking Pouakai Tarns Track (Mangorei Track), winding through lush forests to tussock-covered hilltops and a mirror lake reflecting Mt Taranaki.

5. Savor the flavors of Hawke's Bay wines

Discover New Zealand's oldest wine region in Hawke's Bay. Whether you independently visit wineries for tastings, rent bikes from On Yer Bike Hawkes Bay, or opt for a worry-free tour like Prinsy's Tours, the choice is yours.

6. Catch the sunrise at East Cape

Be one of the first to witness a new day's sunrise in New Zealand, with the iconic East Cape Lighthouse on the easternmost shores of the mainland offering a spectacular view.

7. Beach landing after a thrilling skydive in the Bay of Islands

Combine an adrenaline rush with breathtaking views by taking on a skydiving challenge!

Experience a unique landing on the beach with Skydive Bay of Islands.

8. Follow crystal-clear spring water on the Te Waihou Walkway

Embark on the Te Waihou Walkway to trace the ultra-clear waters of the "Blue Spring." This approximately three-hour walk promises a refreshing journey.

9. Embark on a Whale Watching Cruise

Discover a lesser-known gem for whale watching on the North Island with Auckland Whale and Dolphin Safari. Spot Bryde's whales, bottlenose dolphins, and various seabirds right out of Auckland.

10. Explore the Te Papa Museum

Situated in the capital city, Te Papa is the national museum of New Zealand. Dive into exhibits showcasing the country's volcanoes, flora and fauna, Maori and European settlers, and more. Plus, entry is free!

CHAPTER 5

FIJI TROPICAL PARADISE OVERVIEW

Fiji, a captivating country and archipelago in the South Pacific Ocean, is a true tropical haven. Nestled around the Koro Sea, approximately 1,300 miles north of Auckland, New Zealand, it comprises about 300 islands and 540 islets scattered across a vast expanse of 1,000,000 square miles. Among these islands, around 100 are inhabited, with the capital, Suva, situated on the southeast coast of the largest island, Viti Levu, also known as Great Fiji.

Fiji's allure lies not only in its geographical charm but also in its rich natural beauty. Pristine palm-fringed beaches with powdery white sand and crystal-clear turquoise waters invite you to indulge in activities like swimming, snorkeling, and sunbathing. Venture inland, and you'll find lush tropical rainforests brimming with exotic birds, orchids, and waterfalls, creating an ideal backdrop for hiking. Below the surface, vibrant coral reefs beckon scuba divers and snorkelers to explore a world teeming with sea turtles, manta rays, and a kaleidoscope of colorful fish.

The activities in Fiji are as diverse as its landscapes. From snorkeling and scuba diving to guided hikes leading to scenic viewpoints and hidden waterfalls, the options are endless. Visiting local Fijian villages provides a glimpse into traditional island culture, while surfing, sailing, kayaking, and sport fishing capitalize on Fiji's ideal weather and pristine waters.

Choosing where to go in Fiji can be challenging given its 300 islands. Some top spots include the Mamanuca Islands, offering idyllic beaches and boutique resorts; the Yasawa Islands, known for sailing, snorkeling, and authentic Fijian villages; Viti Levu, Fiji's largest island with diverse attractions; Vanua Levu, a laid-back island rich in Fijian culture; and Taveuni, dubbed Fiji's Garden Island, famous for nature, hiking, and exceptional diving.

Accommodation options in Fiji cater to various preferences and budgets, ranging from dorms to luxurious overwater bungalows. Resorts, whether family-friendly or adults-only, offer an authentic Fijian experience. Eco-retreats on private island resorts provide a chance to disconnect amid nature.

Fijian culture remains vibrant and unique, blending Melanesian, Polynesian, and British influences. Village life revolves around community, emphasizing warm hospitality. Traditional practices, such as meke dance performances and kava ceremonies, offer visitors a genuine taste of Fijian culture.

Fijian cuisine reflects the abundance of tropical produce and fresh seafood. Staples like cassava, taro root, and coconut complement dishes featuring snapper, tuna, prawns, and lobster. Traditional cooking methods, such as pit-roasting and earth ovens, infuse delightful flavors into meals like Kokoda, a raw fish salad with coconut milk.

Reaching Fiji is typically done through Nadi International Airport on Viti Levu. Local airlines facilitate quick flights between islands, while smaller cruise ships and sailing boat charters offer options for island hopping. Internal flights, ferries, buses, and private transfers make navigating individual islands convenient.

Fiji enjoys a warm tropical climate year-round, with the dry season from May to October and a wetter period from November to April. The months of July through September are popular but come with higher prices and more crowds. May, June, and November offer favorable weather with fewer visitors. Diving is excellent year-round, and surfing peaks from June to August.

Packing for Fiji requires light, breathable clothing, swimwear, reef-safe sunscreen, sunglasses, and a hat. Sturdy walking shoes are essential for hikes, and water shoes come in handy for water activities. A light rain jacket is advisable for brief showers, and mosquito repellent helps ward off insects in the humid climate. Don't forget to pack any necessary medications, toiletries, or electronics.

In conclusion, Fiji, with its swaying palm trees, iridescent lagoons, and warm locals, epitomizes the ultimate tropical paradise. Whether you seek heavenly beaches, immersive cultural experiences, or thrilling adventures, Fiji offers an idyllic island escape. Its lush landscapes and vibrant culture create memories that linger long after you've left. start organizing your trip to this South Pacific haven today!

10 Best all-inclusive resorts in Fiji

The enchanting islands of Fiji conjure images of rugged landscapes, emerald forests, and captivating beaches that have charmed travelers for generations. Yet, beyond its natural allure, Fiji harbors a unique secret—its exceptional all-inclusive resorts. In this comprehensive guide to the finest Fiji retreats, we'll explore top-notch accommodations boasting an array of amenities that redefine the typical island getaway.

1. COMO Laucala Island: Nestled in the azure waters of the South Pacific, COMO Laucala Island offers a pinnacle of luxury envisioned by reclusive billionaire Dietrich Mateschitz. With 25 private villas seamlessly blending into the natural landscape, this resort stands as one of the world's best. Each one, two, or three-bedroom residence comes with a personal butler, housekeeping, and babysitting. Renowned for its commitment to sustainability, COMO Laucala Island is powered by solar energy and emphasizes organic, locally-sourced ingredients in its restaurants. Beyond its eco-friendly ethos, the resort offers a plethora of activities, from aquatic adventures to an 18-hole ocean-view golf course.

2. Namale Resort & Spa: Situated in a world of pure bliss and tranquility, Namale All-Inclusive Resort & Spa immerses guests in the sound of ocean waves, lush rainforests, and breathtaking views. Ideal for both exploration and relaxation, Namale offers spectacular diving, snorkeling, hiking, horseback riding, and indulgent spa experiences. With private villas featuring jacuzzi tubs overlooking the serene surroundings, this adults-only resort provides the perfect setting for an ultimate island escape.

3. VOMO Island Resort: Encompassing the northwestern third of Vomo Island, this resort is a haven for rejuvenation. VOMO Island Resort's Kui Spa, set against a backdrop of barefoot luxury, offers indulgent treatments. Culinary delights, described as 'temptation without the guilt,' feature innovative fusion dishes by Executive Chef Iain Todd. Families adore VOMO for its kids' amenities, including a supervised Kids Village and Baby Butler sitter service. With a commitment to sustainability, VOMO leads initiatives from water bottling to turtle conservation.

4. Kokomo Private Island: Beyond its luxurious accommodations, Kokomo Private Island Resort stands out for its commitment to community development and environmental preservation. With 25 Villas and Residences, direct beach access, and activities ranging from snorkeling to cultural experiences, Kokomo offers an unforgettable tropical experience. The resort's support for sustainable tourism and local communities adds depth to its appeal.

5. Yasawa Island Resort & Spa: Renowned for unparalleled beauty, Yasawa Island Resort & Spa offers 18 private luxury bungalows nestled among palms. With private beaches, a full-service spa, and personalized service, Yasawa stands as a superb all-inclusive retreat. Sustainability is key, ensuring luxury coexists with the preservation of the island's natural beauty and culture.

6. Emaho Sekawa Fiji Luxury Retreat: Located in a lush rainforest, Emaho Sekawa Fiji Luxury Retreat provides an adults-only escape with panoramic ocean views. Three villas, featuring private infinity pools, offer a unique blend of luxury and nature. Activities range from forest hikes to snorkeling pristine coral reefs, all in line with the resort's commitment to sustainable tourism and community development.

7. Nukubati Great Sea Reef: As the first solar-powered resort in the South Pacific, Nukubati Great Sea Reef combines unparalleled access to the Great Sea Reef with sustainable and regenerative tourism. Luxurious accommodation includes a sprawling holiday home with private infinity plunge pools. Rich in cultural experiences and activities, Nukubati caters to a diverse range of guests.

8. Jean-Michel Cousteau Resort: Founded by Jacques Cousteau's son, this resort offers an exceptional vacation with a focus on rejuvenation, authentic cuisine, and cultural immersion. Families enjoy the award-winning Bula Club, while adults indulge in spa treatments or restorative yoga. Cousteau Dive Centre adds a bucket-list-worthy underwater adventure.

9. Tadrai Island Resort: An adults-only retreat in the Mamanucas Islands, Tadrai Island Resort provides a luxurious, all-inclusive experience designed exclusively for couples. With five beachfront villas featuring private plunge pools, Pacific Rim cuisine, and a range of activities, Tadrai offers an intimate and eco-friendly vacation.

10. Turtle Island: A couples-only paradise, Turtle Island boasts 14 ultra-lavish beachfront villas overseen by dedicated Bure Mamas. As a leading eco-resort, Turtle Island prioritizes sustainability, supporting local initiatives while providing a luxurious and intimate escape.

These top all-inclusive resorts in Fiji promise not just a getaway but a transformative experience, where luxury harmonizes with nature, and each moment becomes a cherished memory.

What you need to know before going to Fiji

Before traveling to Fiji, here are some essential tips to enhance your experience:

1. Diverse Islands: Fiji is composed of numerous islands, each with its unique charm. Research the main islands like Yasawa, Mamanuca, Taveuni, Viti Levu, Beqa, and

Vanua Levu to tailor your visit to your preferences.

2. Small Resorts and Homestays: For an authentic Fijian experience, opt for smaller resorts and homestays. These accommodations often provide a more immersive cultural experience, including locally made art, guided trips to villages, and Fijian cuisine.

3. Outdoor Adventures: Schedule outdoor activities early in your trip to account for unpredictable tropical weather. Fiji experiences rain and sunshine regardless of forecasts, so planning adventures at the beginning allows flexibility for rescheduling.

4. Duration of Stay: A week allows for a balanced mix of sightseeing and relaxation. If island-hopping, consider the time lost in transit. Slowing down and exploring a few places in-depth is often more rewarding.

5. Bright Clothing: Embrace the vibrant Fijian culture by packing colorful and floral-patterned clothing. From casual beach bars to fine-dining venues, Fijians often dress in bold colors, so feel free to express yourself.

6. Affordable Transportation: Buses and taxis on the main islands are affordable. Public buses are cheaper but stop frequently, while taxis are metered and readily available. Save money by using public transportation for travel within Viti Levu.

7. Bula Spirit: Bula is a common Fijian greeting, reflecting the country's warm hospitality. Learn a few Fijian words, and don't hesitate to engage with the locals. Fijians are forgiving of cultural missteps.

8. Village Etiquette: When entering a village, bring a sevusevu (gift), traditionally kava.

Avoid wearing anything on your head, and dress modestly with a sulu (sarong) and covered shoulders. Follow etiquette during kava ceremonies.

9. Rugby Culture: Rugby is highly cherished in Fiji. Attend a game or watch one at a local bar to engage with the Fijian passion for the sport. It's an excellent conversation starter.

10. Water Safety: Not all tap water is drinkable. Potable water is usually available in Suva, but it's advisable to bring bottled water or use a filter in other areas.

11. Safety in Cities: Exercise caution in cities after dark, as you would in any major city. Keep belongings secure, avoid drinking alone at night, and be cautious around bars, especially in areas like Nadi and Suva.

12. Emergency Contacts: Save emergency contacts such as 911 for emergencies and 917 for police services. In remote areas, seek help from your accommodation or the turaga ni koro (head of the village) if needed.

By being mindful of these tips, you can make the most of your Fijian adventure and immerse yourself in the unique culture and natural beauty that this South Pacific paradise has to offer.

CHAPET 6

PACIFIC ISLANDS

SOLOMON ISLANDS

Things to See & Do

1. Untouched Beauty: Experience the untamed beauty of the Solomon Islands, where rugged landscapes and pristine shores offer an escape from modernity. Explore wild beaches and discover hidden treasures beneath the ocean's surface.

2. World War II Relics: Delve into the remnants of World War II scattered across the islands. Tanks, guns, Japanese bomber planes, and warships serve as historical reminders, particularly from the Guadalcanal Campaign.

3. Cultural Encounters: Immerse yourself in the rich culture of the Solomon Islands through village tours. Learn about traditional daily lives, enjoy local meals, and discover unique customs. Consider staying overnight in rustic settings for a more authentic experience.

4. Diving & Snorkeling: Dive into the crystal-clear waters of the Solomon Islands, known for spectacular reef walls and diverse marine life. Wreck diving is popular due to the islands' World War II history. Snorkelers can also explore shallow waters around some wrecks.

Solomon Islands Culture

1. Diverse Population: Over half a million people inhabit the Solomon Islands, with Melanesian as the predominant ethnicity. The population also includes smaller communities of Polynesians, Micronesians, Chinese, and Europeans.

2. Preservation of Tradition: Solomon Islanders are committed to preserving traditional customs (kastom). The Wantok system emphasizes support within clans or extended families.

3. Rural Living: While the capital, Honiara, is growing, most Solomon Islanders reside in rural villages. Villagers sustain themselves through fishing, hunting, and agriculture. Bartering and alternative currencies, such as shell money, are still practiced.

Things to Know Before Traveling to the Solomon Islands

1. Diverse Islands: Research the main islands such as Yasawa, Mamanuca, Taveuni, Viti Levu, Beqa, and Vanua Levu before arrival.

2. Small Resorts and Homestays: Go for smaller resorts and homestays for a more authentic experience. These accommodations often offer cultural immersion and interactions with locals.

3. Outdoor Adventures: Schedule outdoor activities at the beginning of your trip to account for unpredictable tropical weather.

4. Duration of Stay: A week allows for a balanced mix of sightseeing and relaxation. Consider day trips from your accommodation rather than frequent changes of location.

5. Bright Clothing: Embrace the vibrant Fijian culture by packing colorful and floral-patterned clothing.

6. Affordable Transportation: Buses and taxis on the main islands are affordable. Public buses and metered taxis are common.

7. Bula Spirit: Learn a few Fijian words like "bula" (hello), "vinaka" (thank you), and "moce" (see you later). Embrace the warm hospitality of the Fijian people.

8. Village Etiquette: When entering a village, bring a sevusevu (gift). Follow dress codes, and avoid wearing anything on your head.

9. Rugby Culture: Rugby is highly cherished in Fiji. Attend a game or watch a match to connect with locals.

10. Water Safety: Not all tap water is drinkable. Bring bottled water or use a filter.

11. Safety in Cities: Exercise caution in cities after dark. Follow standard safety precautions.

12. Emergency Contacts: Save emergency contacts, such as 911, for assistance on major islands. Seek help from accommodation or the head of the village in remote areas.

French Polynesia
Things to See & Do

1. Authentic Exploration: Move away from resorts to explore the forests, villages, and remote corners for a more authentic experience in French Polynesia.

2. Diverse Archipelago: French Polynesia's volcanic archipelago comprises 118 islands, each offering a unique tropical landscape. Venture into forests, visit sacred stone sites, and experience traditional ceremonies.

3. History & Culture: Explore the rich history and diverse culture of French Polynesia. Visit archaeological sites, museums, and local pearl farms. Delve into the country's past through unique handicrafts and traditional ceremonies.

4. Swimming with Humpbacks: From August to October, swim with humpback whales around Moorea. Experience the incredible sight of mother and calf, guided by naturalists or wildlife photographers.

5. Small Ship Cruising: Explore the coves and reefs of French Polynesia through small ship cruising. These ships offer access to off-the-beaten-path destinations and insights into the local economy.

6. Hiking: French Polynesia's volcanic landscape provides excellent hiking trails with ocean views, secret beachside paths, and archaeological sites. Trails on Fatu Hiva and Atuona offer breathtaking views.

French Polynesia Culture

1. Migration History: French Polynesia's first inhabitants migrated from Southeast Asia around 4,000 years ago. European explorers arrived in the 16th century, and the islands were colonized by the French in the mid-19th century.

2. Cultural Diversity: The majority of residents is of Polynesian or mixed Polynesian ethnicity. French is the official language, and Christianity is the main religion. Traditional ceremonies, handicrafts, and carvings vary across islands.

Kiribati

Things to See & Do

1. Remote Paradise: Kiribati, one of the world's smallest and least-visited island nations, offers a remote and idyllic destination. With only around 6,000 visitors annually, the untouched beauty of Kiribati provides a castaway experience without the typical tourist crowds.

2. Water and Land Ratio: Kiribati's vast spread of 33 islands over 3.5 million sq km gives it the world's largest water-to-land ratio. Kiritimati (Christmas Island), the largest coral atoll, is a key attraction for tourists, despite being approximately 5,000km from any other nation.

3. Cultural Immersion: Explore the unique culture of Kiribati, with Te Katei ni Kiribati (the Kiribati way of life) illustrated through traditional meeting houses (maneaba) where community decisions are made. Family ties, social obligations, and hospitality are highly valued.

4. Activities: Engage in various activities, from snorkeling, diving, and fishing to bird watching. Kiribati's low-lying atolls and turquoise lagoons offer excellent opportunities for water-based pursuits.

Things to Know Before Traveling to Kiribati

1. Limited Visitors: Due to its remote location, Kiribati is challenging to reach, making it suitable for organized, multi-country small group expeditions. Independent travel or short one-stop trips may not be well-suited.

2. Village Tours: Inject cultural experiences into your visit by spending time in Kiribati villages. Learn traditional skills, hear old legends, and experience the warmth of local hospitality.

3. Diving & Snorkeling: Explore the brilliant turquoise lagoon in North Tarawa through activities like diving, snorkeling, and canoeing. Kiritimati offers opportunities for fishing with marlin, wahoo, barracuda, and large tuna.

4. Bird Watching: Discover Kiribati's thriving bird population, including seabirds like boobies, petrels, and gulls. In forested areas, observe land-based birds like the Pacific long-tailed cuckoo and the endemic Christmas Island warbler.

5. War History: Learn about Kiribati's role in World War II by visiting South Tarawa. Explore sites, memorials, and hear stories about the impact of the war on the country.

Micronesia

Culture & History

1. Geographical Spread: The Federated States of Micronesia comprises 607 small islands, located about 4,000km southwest of Hawaii. Despite a total land area of 700km2 and a population of 111,000, Micronesia spans two time zones and occupies an area of Pacific Ocean five times the size of France.

2. Cultural Diversity: Micronesia's four states have distinct cultures and traditions, emphasizing the importance of extended family and clan systems. The predominant religion is Christianity, with diverse denominations represented.

3. Historical Background: Micronesia has a history of foreign rule, including Spanish, German, and Japanese occupations. Japanese settlement during the 1920s and 1930s influenced the country's role in World War II, with remnants visible in Chuuk Lagoon. The elderly population often speaks fluent Japanese.

Things to Do in Micronesia

1. Tour Pohnpei: Explore Micronesia's most populous island, Pohnpei, on a guided tour. Visit a pepper farm, freshwater eel farm, waterfalls, the government seat at Palikir, and the village of Kapinga. Experience local legends, traditional handicrafts, and mysterious sites like Pwisehn Malek.

2. Diving & Snorkeling: With more ocean than land, Micronesia offers spectacular underwater sights. Explore colorful reefs, encounter manta rays and sharks, and dive into Chuuk's Truk Lagoon, home to numerous shipwrecks from World War II.

3. Archaeological Sites: Gain insights into Micronesia's history through ancient ruins.

Visit the stone city of Nan Madol on Pohnpei, dating back 1,000 years, accessible only by boat. Explore the Lelu Ruins on Kosrae, remnants of a walled city from the 12th century.

4. Join a Tour: Due to the difficulty of independent travel, consider joining a small group tour. Experienced guides enhance your experience, helping you explore multiple countries in the region.

Micronesia and Kiribati offer unique experiences, from remote paradise in Kiribati to the cultural and historical diversity of Micronesia. Whether you seek untouched beauty, water adventures, or a journey into history, these Pacific destinations promise unforgettable moments.

CHAPTER 7

CULTURAL ETIQUETTE AND RESPECT IN OCEANIA COUNTRIES

Australia - Culture, Etiquette, and Practices

Languages in Australia are:

1. English Dominance: While English is the primary language, Australians have a unique vocabulary, accent, and slang known as 'Strine,' reflecting their distinctive way of speaking.

2. Aboriginal Languages: Historically, there were 250 Aboriginal languages; however, only 20 survive today, mainly in remote regions. Efforts are made to revive and promote indigenous languages.

3. Multilingual Society: Apart from English, languages spoken include Mandarin, Cantonese, Vietnamese, Italian, Greek, Arabic, Hindi, Punjabi, and others. Over 20% speak a language other than English at home, highlighting Australia's multiculturalism.

Australian Society & Culture

1. Aussie Modesty: Australians value humility, authenticity, and informality. They appreciate sincerity and humor while disliking pretentiousness. Deprecatory comments are a sign of friendship, and banter and sarcasm are common.

2. Relationships - Mates: Relationships emphasize equality, and Australians are loyal to friends. They value authenticity over wealth or status, and boasting about achievements is frowned upon.

3. Multicultural Society: Australia is multicultural, with indigenous groups,

European roots, and diverse immigrant populations. Approximately 25% of Australians were born overseas, creating a shift towards a multi-cultural identity.

Australian Etiquette & Customs

1. Meeting Etiquette: Greetings are casual; handshakes, smiles, and a simple 'hello' are common. Australians prefer using first names, and titles are usually avoided. Tactile gestures are acceptable among close friends.

2. Gift Giving: Small, modest gifts are exchanged on special occasions. High-value gifts may be perceived as flaunting wealth. Cash gifts are rare, and gifts are typically opened when received.

3. Dining Etiquette: BBQs (barbies) are significant social events. Guests often bring wine or beer for personal consumption. Dress codes vary, but Australians tend to be casual.

Arrive on time, offer help to hosts, and be prepared to split bills in restaurants.

Australia's culture reflects values of humility, equality, and authenticity, making it a diverse and welcoming society. Understanding local etiquette enhances interactions and fosters positive relationships.

New Zealand - Culture, Etiquette, and Practices

Languages in New Zealand are:

1. English, Maori, and NZ Sign Language: New Zealand has three official languages. English is the language of day-to-day business, while Maori is a Polynesian language, recognized since the Maori Language Act of 1987. NZ Sign Language is also an official language.

Kiwi Society & Culture

1. Demeanor: New Zealanders (Kiwis) are friendly, outgoing, and reserved initially. They value hospitality and quickly move to a first-name basis. Kiwis dress casually, reflecting a generally informal culture.

2. Environmentalism: Kiwis are environmentally concerned, influenced by the Maori belief in 'mauri' (life force). Damage to the environment affects the vitality of the mauri, emphasizing the importance of preserving the environment.

3. Egalitarianism: New Zealand has no formal class structure. Kiwis take pride in individual achievements, and wealth and social status are less important. The country follows a 'welfare state' model, providing benefits to those in need.

Etiquette and Manners in New Zealand

1. Meeting and Greeting: Greetings are casual with a handshake and a smile. Kiwis quickly move to first-name basis. It's advisable to address people by their honorific title and surname until a more familiar level is suggested.

2. Maori Meeting and Greeting: Maori follow distinct protocols, especially during a Powhiri - a formal welcome. The Powhiri involves speeches, songs, and specific seating arrangements. Visitors are expected to have a speaker reply on their behalf.

3. Gift Giving Etiquette: Bring small gifts like flowers, chocolates, or a book when invited to a Kiwi's house. Gifts should not be lavish, and they are opened when received.

4. Dining Etiquette: New Zealanders are casual, but more formal occasions have stricter protocols. Meals are often served family-style. Table manners are Continental, but Kiwis are tolerant of different manners. Maori dining etiquette involves waiting for food acknowledgment, allowing home people to sit amongst visitors, and thanking volunteers serving the meal.

Understanding New Zealand's cultural nuances, including Maori protocols, enhances interactions and fosters positive relationships in various settings, from casual meetings to formal events.

CONCLUSION

As we reach the final pages of the Oceania Travel Guide 2024, it's like saying goodbye to an old friend. This guide has been more than just a bunch of travel tips; it's been a companion, telling stories and opening doors to the wonders of the Pacific.

We've strolled through the coral reefs of the Great Barrier Reef and marveled at the volcanic landscapes of New Zealand. Each chapter was a new adventure, giving us a taste of the diverse cultures and breathtaking natural beauty that make Oceania so special.

But beyond the places, this guide has introduced us to the incredible people who call Oceania home. Their resilience and commitment to preserving their traditions in the face of change is nothing short of inspiring. The stories shared here are a tribute to these communities and their role in shaping the identity of Oceania.

As we close the book, there's a call for us to be mindful travelers. Let's cherish and respect the environment, leaving behind only footprints and taking with us a deeper understanding of the delicate balance between nature and culture.

The guide encourages us to be ambassadors of goodwill, fostering a spirit of responsible and sustainable travel. It's a reminder that our journey doesn't truly end – it becomes a part of the collective memory of those who have been enchanted by the magic of Oceania.

So, here's to the travelers who will follow in our footsteps. May they be inspired by the tales shared in these pages and find their own unique adventure in the vast blue expanse of Oceania. As we say farewell, it's not goodbye but a 'see you later' to the enchanting world of

Oceania. Safe travels and may the Pacific breeze guide you on your next great adventure.

Printed in Great Britain
by Amazon

41923648R00076